Dog Treats

Recipe Book

A Dog Treats Cookbook With 75 Homemade, Healthy, Delicious And Fun Treats For Your Dog

HEIDI GREEN

ISBN: 9798827476559

DEDICATION

To all dog lovers out there.

TABLE OF CONTENTS

INTRODUCTION

The right diet is an important aspect of loving and caring for your dog. It gives them energy and enhances overall wellbeing. People who want to be healthy do their best to eat healthy food that are not highly-processed or filled with excess preservatives. We know that these types of food or snacks are not good for our bodies and we avoid them as much as we can. We should also do the same for our dogs if we really love them.

For dogs to live their best lives, we must be intentional about what they eat. Their food must be full of the right type of nutrients. Healthy food will give them energy and boost their immunity to fight off diseases. A well-fed dog will also be a better companion to you.

Treats are an essential part of what dogs eat and they should not be taken for granted. Dogs will be much healthier if we make the effort to ensure that they are given treats that have high nutritional value. Incorporating healthy treats into the diet of dogs will transform their health and overall wellbeing. They will have more energy, stronger teeth, cleaner breathe and healthier fur.

In the past, it was okay to give your dog any food or treat that is at hand but this is no longer so. Feeding your pet is no longer as simple as it was. Many of the readily available store-bought dog treats are or doubtful origin. They may contain addictives, preservatives and other chemicals that are harmful. This is why many pet lovers are turning to homemade dog treats. Homemade dog treats are easy to make, they are healthy and are the best rewards for your pet.

The Dangers Of Commercial Dog Treats

Over the years, many pet owners have had to spend a lot of money taking care of sick dogs. From allergic reactions to organ failures – a great number of these sicknesses were traced to commercial dog food or treats. Many commercial dog foods were found to contain addictives and toxins that are outrightly dangerous to dogs. These were the causes of the sickness in the dogs.

Apart from harmful ingredients, some commercial dog treats are made under unhygienic conditions. Mold, metals, harmful bacteria and other toxic items can easily get into dog treats when the proper standards are not adhered to. Some of these treats are also fattening and can make dogs become obese.

All these can be avoided if you take the time to make DIY treats for your dog. Homemade treats are safe and can be made as healthy as you want. You know what your dogs like and what is good for their health. Making dog treats from scratch ensures that they are made with only the healthiest ingredients. You are completely in control of the preparation process. There are no chemicals or preservatives – you are in total control and determine the ingredients that go in and those that stay out.

Apart from avoiding the risk of sickness and allergic reactions, homemade dog treats also helps you to find the right treats for dogs that are picky eaters. These DIY treats are also budget friendly and are made with ingredients that are already available in most homes.

Using This Book

This book has solved for you the problem of finding appropriate and safe treats for your dog. The 75 recipes cover a variety of treats for all types of dog diets and taste preferences. There is no one-size-fits-all dog treat recipe. The diet and nutritional requirements of dogs vary with breed and age.

Take time to prepare these treats one by one and give them to your dog. Pay attention your dogs as they eat each treat so you can determine the one that they like most. If you already know the foods that your dog does not like then either skip the recipes that contains those ingredients or find the appropriate ingredient substitute.

It is best to prepare a batch of 2 to 3 of these treats at a time. This enables you to have a variety of treats to give to your dog whenever you like. Remember to store them properly in airtight containers and refrigerate or freeze as required. Only take out what you need for the day. Mixing up the treats is also great for creating a balance in the dog's diet. Treats are an important part of the nutrition of dogs and should help them to be healthy and energetic.

This book does not constitute the advice of a veterinarian. If you are not sure of any dietary ingredient or changes, check with your veterinarian. You should also obtain information about any food allergies and sensitivities your dog may have.

Safe Human Food That Are Toxic To Dogs

Do not take the short cut to giving treats to your dogs by just throwing to them whatever you have at hand. Just because you can eat something does not mean your dog can eat it. Many cooked or uncooked food that are safe for human consumption are toxic to dogs. Some of these items do not contain toxins but cause other gastrointestinal troubles for dogs.

Not only should you not give these items to your dogs, you should also make sure they are safely stored in places your dogs cannot get to. Here is a list of food items that are not good for dogs:

Avocados,

Apricot Pits,

Apple Seeds,

Cherry Pits,

Limes, lemon,

Alcohol,

Caffeine,

Bread, pizza and other pastry dough,

Chocolate,

Corn on the Cob,

Raw fish,

Raisins,

Grapes,

Macadamia nuts and butters,

Onions, chives, garlic

Pits and seeds eg from pear, persimmon and plum,

Xylitol,

Processed Foods that contain any of the above.

Safety Tips For Making Dog Treats

Don't have your dog in the kitchen while making treats or cooking any food. They can be hurt by hot stoves and ovens.

Do not use containers and baking molds that contain BPA. They have been linked to cancer and other health problems.

Avoid toxic ingredients (see list in the previous section.) Read labels on all products carefully to be sure they don't contain any ingredients that are unsafe for dogs.

Use organic ingredients as much as you can.

Maintain proper hygiene to avoid contaminating the treats you make.

All the best!

NO BAKE TREATS

Coconut Ball

This is good for reducing any fleas, allergies in dogs.

Preparation time: 10 minutes

Cooking time: 0 minutes

Servings: 5

Ingredients:

2 - 3 tablespoons peanut butter

1/3 cup coconut, grated or finely shredded

1/3 cup coconut oil

2 1/2 cups rolled oats

Directions:

1. Combine rolled oats, coconut oil, peanut butter into a bowl or food processor, mix until well combined.

2. Using a spoon, scoop out bite-sized pieces and roll into a ball with hands.

3. Gently toss each of the balls in grated coconut until well coated.

4. Line a flat tray with baking paper and place the coated balls on it.

5. Put into refrigerator for 30 minutes.

5. Serve.

No-Bake Peanut Butter Dog Treat

This is a yummy treat to give your best friend.

Preparation Time: 5 minutes

Cooking time: 0 minutes

Servings: 4

Ingredients:

1/4 cup blueberries

2 cup rolled oats

1 tablespoon coconut oil

1/2 cup unsweetened peanut butter

1/2 cup unsweetened applesauce

Directions:

1. Mix peanut butter, applesauce, coconut oil, and blueberries stir until properly combined.

2. Add the oat into the mixture and stir.

3. Scoop up mixture with a tablespoon and roll into a ball with hand.

4. Dust rolled balls with more oats

5. Refrigerate for an hour.

6. Bring out treats and serve.

Cranberries & Apple Treat

Cranberries are known to help improve dog immune system and bladder health.

Preparation time: 10 minutes

Cooking time: 0 minute

Servings: 8

Ingredients:

6 heaped tablespoons of quick oats, divided

2 tablespoons cranberries, dried

1/4 of a large apple, grated

1 tablespoon water

Directions:

1. Chop up 4 tablespoons of oats in a food processor.

2. Add cranberries to the ground oats and grind into small pieces.

3. Add grated apple and the remaining oats to the mixture, mix with your hand. If needed, add a little water to ensure the mixture sticks together.

4. Roll mixture into balls with hands.

5. Refrigerate.

Pumpkin Dog Treats

This helps to moisturize your dog's skin and coat.

Preparation time: 5 minutes

Cooking time: 0 minutes

Servings: 8

Ingredients:

1/2 cup peanut butter

2 1/2 cup rolled oats

1 cup pumpkin puree

1 teaspoon cinnamon

1/4 cup honey

Directions:

1. Stir all the ingredients together in a bowl until thoroughly combined.

2. Form the mixture into 1 1/2 inch balls.

3. Place on a baking sheet lined with parchment paper.

4. Refrigerate for an hour.

5. Serve your pup.

6. Store in airtight containers.

Coconut Peanut Butter Dog Treat

This helps to improve your pup's eyesight.

Preparation time: 5 minutes

Cooking time: 0 minute

Servings: 5

Ingredients:

1/2 cup peanut butter

1/2 cup coconut oil

1/4 teaspoon turmeric, optional

1/4 teaspoon cinnamon, optional

Directions:

1. Whisk all the ingredients together in a small saucepan on low heat until slightly melted. Stir in optional ingredients if using.

2. Put the mixture into silicone molds and fill just over halfway.

3. Freeze for 25 minutes and ensure the molds are on a flat surface for even freezing.

4. Once hardened, transfer to a freezer bag and freeze.

Blueberry Yoghurt Dog Treat

This is an energizing treat for dogs.

Preparation time: 5 minutes

Cooking time: 0 minute

Servings: 10

Ingredients:

3/4 cup blueberries, fresh (thaw first if using frozen)

6 tablespoons Greek yoghurt

Directions:

1. Plat the silicon mold on a small flat tray.

2. Divide the yoghurt between the molds and flatten the top. Freeze for 20 minutes.

3. In a blender, blend your blueberries until smooth.

4. Remove the yoghurt from the freezer and using a small spoon top each mold with the blended blueberries.

5. Freeze for another 40 minutes to an hour, until solid

6. Transfer to a freezer baggie, seal and store in the freezer for up to months.

Carrot Peanut Butter Puppy Bites

This helps dogs to maintain regular digestion.

Preparation time: 5 minutes

Cooking time: 0 minute

Servings: 10

Ingredients:

6 tablespoons unsweetened applesauce

2 carrots, sliced into 1/2-inch slices

¼ cup wheat bran

½ cup peanut butter

2/3 cup rolled oats

Directions:

1. Mix the wheat bran, applesauce, peanut butter, and rolled oats in a large bowl until well combined.

2. Scoop a heaped tablespoon of the mixture and roll into a ball using your hand.

3. Push a carrot slice into the middle of the ball and form the mixture into a patty surrounding the carrot. Repeat until the mixture and carrot slices are used up. This makes about 24.

4. Refrigerate or freeze in an airtight container. It can stay in the fridge for 2 weeks and in the freezer for up to 2 months.

Banana Peanut Butter Treat

Give this to dogs that need to add healthy weight.

Preparation time: 5 minutes

Cooking time: 0 minute

Servings: 8

Ingredients:

1 banana, mashed

1 tablespoon honey

1 teaspoon cinnamon

3/4 cup oatmeal

1/2 cup peanut butter

1 cup unsweetened shredded coconut (optional)

Directions:

1. Mix together all the ingredients, except the coconut, in a large bowl. Stir well.

2. Oil your hands then scoop up a heaped tablespoon of the mixture and roll into a ball or any preferred shape using hands.

3. Roll the ball in shredded coconut to coat. Continue until the ingredients are exhausted.

4. Refrigerate until firm and store in airtight container in the fridge for up to 1 week. You can freeze for 2-3 months.

BISCUITS AND SNACKS

Pumpkin Apple Dog Biscuit

This is a treat that is full of nutrients.

Preparation time: 10 minutes

Cooking time: 30 minutes

Servings: 6

Ingredients:

2 1/3 cups whole wheat flour, divided

1/2 cup pumpkin puree

1 small apple, core removed, grated

1/2 cup water

1 egg

1 teaspoon baking powder

Directions:

1. Preheat oven to 375°F.

2. Line two baking sheets with parchment paper.

3. In a bowl, thoroughly mix baking powder and 2 cups of flour.

4. Add the remaining ingredients and mix until they are thoroughly combined. If the dough is sticky, gradually add the reserved 1/3 cup of flour and knead it into it until it is no longer sticky.

5. Lightly flour a surface and roll out the dough on it.

6. Using a cookie cutter or dog biscuit cookie cutter, cut dough to preferred shape, and place on baking sheet.

7. Bake for 30 minutes or until crisp.

8. Allow to cool before serving. Store in an airtight container.

Buttery Milk Dog Biscuit

Reduces the occurrence of skin problem and itching.

Preparation Time: 20 minutes

Cooking time: 30 minutes

Servings: 10

Ingredients:

3/4 cup hot beef or chicken broth

1/3 cup margarine

1/2 cup powdered milk

1 egg

3 cups whole wheat flour

A pinch of salt

Directions:

1. Preheat oven to 325° F

2. Line 2 baking sheets with parchment paper.

3. Add the margarine to a large bowl and pour the hot broth on it. Stir in the egg, salt and powdered milk.

4. Add flour a little at a time and knead for while until the dough is stiff.

5. On a smooth surface, roll out the dough to 1/2 – 1/4 inch thickness.

6. Cut to bone shapes or other preferred shapes. Arrange on the prepared baking sheets.

7. Bake for 30 minutes. Leave to cool on a rack.

Oats Carrot Dog Biscuit

This is a treat that dogs can never get tired of.

Preparation time: 5 minutes

Cooking time: 25 minutes

Servings: 25

Ingredients:

1 large egg or 1/4 cup unsweetened applesauce

1 tablespoon baking powder

1/2 cup quick or whole-rolled oats

3/4 cup water or broth

2/3 cup shredded carrot

2 1/4 cups whole wheat flour

1 cup peanut butter

Directions:

1. Preheat oven to 325°F.

2. Slowly mix egg, peanut butter, water and carrot in a large bowl with either a rubber spatula or wooden spoon.

3. Add flour and oats then knead with hand until it forms a heavy and thick dough.

4. Roll dough on a smooth surface into 1/4 inch thickness using a floured rolling pin.

5. Cut into desired shape using a cookie cutter or sharp knife.

6. Place treats on baking sheet lined with parchment paper.

7. Bake for 15 minutes or until browned lightly at the bottom.

8. Flip and bake on the other side for additional 10 minutes.

9. Allow to cool before serving.

Carrot Apple Dog Biscuit

This biscuit contains antioxidants that improve the immune system.

Preparation time: 5 minutes

Cooking time: 40 minutes

Servings: 20

Ingredients:

1/3 cup vegetable oil

1/2 cup peeled and grated carrot

1 large egg, whisked

1/2 cup oats

2 1/2 cups whole wheat flour

1 apple, cored, grated

1/4 -1/2 cup water

1 tablespoon brown sugar, optional

Directions:

1. Preheat oven to 350°F.

2. Coat a cookie sheet with cooking spray and set aside.

3. In a large bowl, mix the oats, flour, and sugar, set aside.

4. In a separate large bowl, mix egg, water, oil and apple until thoroughly combined.

5. Add the wet ingredients to the dry ingredients and completely mix together.

6. Roll out dough carefully.

7. Use a sharp knife or cookie cutter to cut to preferred shape.

8. Bake for 40-45 minutes or until biscuits are hardened. Then allow to cool.

9. Store in airtight container.

Easy Peanut Butter Dog Biscuit

This treat makes for happy dogs.

Preparation time: 2 minutes

Cooking time: 14 minutes

Servings: 7

Ingredients:

1 cup rolled oats

1 cup chicken broth

1 tablespoon coconut oil

1/2 cup peanut butter

1/4 cup honey

1 cup all-purpose flour

1 cup whole wheat flour

Directions:

1. Preheat oven to 350°F.

2. Mix the honey, oil, broth, and peanut butter in a bowl until well combined.

3. In a separate bowl mix oats, wheat and all-purpose flour.

4. Next, mix the wet ingredients and dry ingredients together thoroughly.

5. Dust a surface with flour and roll out the dough to 1/4-inch thickness.

6. Use a cookie cutter to cut to preferred shape. Roll together leftovers and cut out as well.

7. Place cut-out dough on a baking sheet lined with two parchment papers.

8. Bake for 14-16 minutes.

9. Allow to cool before storing in an airtight container. It can stay good for a week at room temperature and longer in the fridge.

Bacon Wheat Biscuit

This is good for greedy pups. It fills them up quickly.

Preparation time: 20 minutes

Cooking time: 40 minutes

Servings: 20

Ingredients:

10 tablespoons melted bacon fat

1/2 cup water

1 cup milk

5 cups of whole wheat flour

1 teaspoon salt

2 large eggs, beaten

Directions:

1. Preheat your oven to 350°F.

2. Spray cooking spray on a cookie sheet.

3. Mix the bacon fat, water, egg, milk and salt in a large bowl until properly blended and smooth.

4. Slowly stir in flour until it makes a stiff dough.

5. Roll the dough into 2-inch balls.

6. Bake for 35–40 minutes.

7. Transfer to racks and leave to cool. Cover in a container and store in your fridge.

Easiest Puppy Biscuit

This is as easy as the name.

Preparation time: 15 minutes

Cooking time: 20 minutes

Servings: 25

Ingredients:

2 large eggs, lightly whisked

3 cups whole wheat flour

1/3 – 1/2 cup water

Directions:

1. Preheat oven to 350°F.

2. Mix everything together in a large bowl, stir until thoroughly combined and dough is formed.

3. Sprinkle a surface with flour and roll out dough to about 1/4 inch thickness.

4. Using a cookie cutter, cut to preferred shape.

5. Place on baking sheet lined with parchment paper.

6. Bake for 18-20 minutes or until the treat is golden.

7. Transfer to racks and leave to cool. Cover in an airtight container and store for up to two weeks in your fridge.

Yeast Biscuit

Helps control fleas and other pests in dogs.

Preparation time: 30 minutes

Cooking time: 40 minutes

Servings: 10

Ingredients:

1/2 cup brewer's yeast

1 cup chicken broth

3 tablespoons vegetable oil

2 1/2 cups whole wheat flour

Directions:

1. Preheat oven to 375°F.

2. Add all ingredients to a large bowl and stir thoroughly until well combined.

3. Roll out the dough on floured surface to 1/4 inch thickness.

4. Cut the dough into preferred shape with 3-inch cookie cutter.

5. Place treats on 2 ungreased cookie sheets.

6. Bake for 40 minutes until crunchy and browned.

7. Allow to cool and serve. Cover in an airtight container and store for up to two weeks

NUTS & SEEDS

Sunflower Seed Dog Treat

This contains fatty acids which are proven to improve the skin and coat of dogs.

Preparation time: 5 minutes

Cooking time: 25 minutes

Servings: 6

Ingredients:

3/4 cup cranberries, dried

1/4 cup of maple syrup

1 egg

2 - 3 tablespoons cold water

1 1/4 cup of whole grain oat flour

1/4 cup ground flaxseed

3/4 cup unsalted sunflower seed, shell removed

1/2 cup rolled oats

1 cup brown rice flour

5 tablespoons applesauce

Directions:

1. Preheat oven to 350°F.

2. Add all the dry ingredients to a large bowl and mix them together with a wooden spoon.

3. Add the maple syrup, egg and applesauce to the dry ingredients, mixing thoroughly until dough is formed. Knead for a while with your hands.

4. If the dough is too dry, add a tablespoon of water at a time to make it more sticky.

5. Roll out dough on a floured surface to 1/4 inch thickness,

6. Using a cookie cutter cut dough into preferred shapes and place on a baking sheet lined with parchment paper.

7. Bake treats for 25 minutes.

8. Allow to cool and store in an airtight jar. It can stay in the fridge for up to 1 week.

Hemp Seed Biscuits

These are good for strong joints and healthy skin.

Preparation time: 45 minutes

Cooking time: 30 minutes

Servings:

Ingredients:

1 1/2 cups brown rice flour

1/3 cup hemp seeds

1/2 cup unsweetened applesauce

1/4 coconut oil, melted

Directions:

1. In a bowl, combine all the ingredients and mix together.

2. Knead until everything comes together to form dough ball. Place in the fridge for 30 minutes to harden a bit.

3. On a floured surface, roll the dough out to 1/4 inch thick. Cut into dog bone shape or simply rectangles.

4. Arrange the treats on a baking sheet with space in between them.

5. Bake for 30 minutes at 350°F or until cooked through and hard.

Nut Butter Treats

This treat contains essential nutrients and minerals to boost your dog immune system.

Preparation time: 5 minutes

Cooking time: 15 minutes

Servings: 10

Ingredients:

1/4 cup mashed banana

1/4 cup beef or chicken stock

1 cup whole wheat flour

1/2 cup preferred nut butter

Directions:

1. Preheat oven to 350°F.

2. In a large mixing bowl, combine all ingredients until a thick dough is formed.

3. Roll dough on smooth surface until it is 1/4 thick.

4. Using a cookie cutter, cut into preferred shape.

5. Bake for 15 – 20 minutes until treat turns golden brown.

Fennel Seed Dog Treat

This contains calcium, iron, vitamin A and C that helps with digestion, bad breath, and gassiness.

Preparation time: 5 minutes

Cooking time: 25 minutes

Servings: 9

Ingredients:

1/2 cup shredded carrot

1 1/2 tablespoons fennel seeds

1/2 cup shredded zucchini

2/3 cup flax seed meal

1 cup brown rice flour

2 medium eggs

1 teaspoon baking powder

Directions:

1. Preheat oven to 350°F.

2. Use parchment paper to line a baking pan.

3. In a large bowl, mix the flax meal, fennel seeds, baking powder and flour until they are thoroughly properly combined.

4. Add zucchini and carrot; stir properly.

5. Add the eggs and knead with hands until dough is formed.

6. On a flat surface, place dough between two saran wraps and roll out to preferred thickness.

7. Using a sharp knife or cookie cutter, cut dough into preferred shape and place on the prepared pan.

8. Bake for 25 minutes.

9. Transfer to racks and leave to cool. Store in a covered airtight container.

Chia Seed Treats

This helps in blood sugar regulation.

Preparation time: 10 minutes

Cooking time: 30 minutes

Servings: 5

Ingredients:

2 tablespoons olive oil

1 1/2 cup of beef broth

2 cups whole wheat flour

3 tablespoons of chia seed, ground

3 tablespoons water

Directions:

1. Preheat oven to 300°F.

2. Mix chia seed with water in a small bowl then allow to sit for 30 seconds.

3. In the bowl of a stand mixer, combine the soaked chia seed, flour and oil.

4. Slowly add in the beef broth until dough is formed (you may not need to add the entire 1 1/2 cups).

5. Lightly flour a surface and roll out dough on it,

6. Cut dough into preferred shape with cookie cutter and place on a baking sheet lined with parchment paper.

7. Bake for 30 minutes. Let them be completely cooled before serving.

Honey Nuts Waffle

Boosts energy level and aids digestion.

Preparation time: 10 minutes

Cooking time: 20 minutes

Servings: 6

Ingredients:

2 tablespoons coconut oil

1/3 cup Greek yogurt

1/2 cup oat flour

2 tablespoons honey

1/4 cup peanut butter

1 egg

Directions:

1. Preheat oven to 350°F.

2. Mix all ingredients into your blender then blend until smooth.

3. Pour the mixture into a silicon waffle mold.

4. Bake for 20 to 30 minutes.

5. Allow to cool, serve dog or keep in an airtight container.

Aniseed Dog Treats

This helps with digestive issues that cause gas and tiredness in dogs.

Preparation time: 5 minutes

Cooking time: 25 minutes

Servings: 10

Ingredients:

1 tablespoon aniseed, crushed roughly

2 eggs

4 1/2 tablespoons peanut butter

1 medium-sized sweet potato

3 cups whole wheat flour

Directions:

1. Preheat oven to 350°F.

2. Using a fork, prick all over the potato then microwave for about 6 – 8 minutes until soft. Allow to cool then discard the skin and scoop out flesh.

3. Using an electric mixer, stir the potato, peanut butter and eggs together.

4. Slowly add in flour and combine until dough is not sticky (you may not use up the entire 3 cups).

5. Add aniseed and mix.

6. Sprinkle flour on a smooth surface and roll out dough to 1/4 inch thickness.

7. Using a cookie cutter, cut out treats, and place on baking sheet lined with parchment paper.

8. Bake for 25 - 30 minutes or until edges turn golden.

FRUITY TREATS

Frozen Yogurt Watermelon Treats
It's packed with high level of nutrients and fiber.

Preparation time: 20 minutes

Cooking time: 0 minutes

Servings: 2

Ingredients:

1 1/2 cup seedless watermelon, peeled and diced

1/2 cup plain or Greek yogurt

2 teaspoons honey

Ingredients:

1. Process all ingredients together in a food processor until smooth.

2. Pour mixture into silicon molds.

3. Freeze until firm.

Fruity Parfait
This helps to improve the digestive health of dogs.

Preparation time: 5 minutes

Cooking time: 0 minutes

Servings: 2

Ingredients:

1/2 cup plain yogurt

1/2 cup butternut squash

1/2 cup blueberries

½ cup applesauce

Directions:

1. Put all ingredients into a large bowl and properly stir until well combined.

2. If your dog dislikes eating vegetable or fruit pieces, pour all into a blender and blend until pureed.

3. Serve your dog immediately.

Easy Fruity Dog Treat

Helps to manage dog weight and keep them energized all day.

Preparation time: 30 minutes

Cooking time: 0 minutes

Servings: 4

Ingredients:

2 tablespoon dried cranberries

1/4 red apple, grated

1 tablespoon water

6 tablespoons of oat, divided

Directions:

1. Chop up 4 tablespoons of oats in a food processor.

2. Add cranberries to the oats and process into small pieces.

3. Add the grated apple and remaining oats. Mix thoroughly with hand.

4. Sprinkle with a little water if needed to make it sticky.

5. Form balls of preferred sizes.

6. Store in refrigerator.

Strawberry Banana Smoothie

This is great for keeping your cool in hot weather.

Preparation time: 10 minutes

Cooking time: 0 minutes

Servings: 20

Ingredients:

2 cups strawberries, hull removed, halved

3/4 cup plain Greek yogurt

1/4 cup low fat milk

1 large banana, sliced

Directions:

1. Blend all ingredients until the mixture is smooth.

2. Pour mixture into a silicone mold or paper cups.

3. Freeze for 6 hours.

4. Remove treat place in freezer bag.

5. Store in freezer. Serve frozen.

Frozen Fruit Yogurt

This is high in protein and calcium that keeps your pup's bones healthy.

Preparation time: 5 minutes

Cooking time: 0 minutes

Servings: 12

Ingredients:

2 cups Greek yogurt

4/5 cup of water

Dog-friendly fruits like apple, mango, strawberry, banana, raspberry, watermelon, and peach.

Directions:

1. Clean the fruits chop into smaller pieces.

2. Fill the silicone mold up to 1/3 with yogurt. Splash a little water on top then add some fruit pieces.

3. Again, start with yogurt and repeat this layering until the molds are full.

4. Once done, place the mold in the freezer for 4 to 5 hours.

6. Thaw for about 5 – 10 minutes before serving.

Fruity Dog Treat

This contains Omega fatty acids that help to maintain your pup's fur and skin.

Preparation time: 5 minutes

Cooking time: 25 minutes

Servings: 3

Ingredients:

1 cup of carrot, grated finely

1/4 cup unsweetened applesauce

2 tablespoons water

1 cup oats

1 banana, mashed

1 1/2 cups whole wheat flour

Directions:

1. Preheat oven to 350°F.

2. Combine grated carrot, banana, applesauce and water.

3. Stir in the oats and slowly add the flour until the dough forms.

4. Sprinkle a smooth surface with flour then roll out dough to 1/2 inch thickness

5. Use a cookie cutter to cut out dough into 1-inch pieces, and place on a greased cookie sheet.

6. Bake for 25 minutes. Switch off the oven and leave the cookies there for 1-2 hours before removing. This will make them chewier.

Tropical Frozen Yogurt Treat

Maintains and strengthens dogs' teeth.

Preparation time: 10 minutes

Cooking time: 0 minutes

Servings: 5

Ingredients:

1 cup low fat Greek yogurt

1 ripe banana, peeled, cut into pieces

I large mango, peeled, seeded, cut into pieces

Directions:

1. Put all ingredients into your blender and blend until smooth.

2. Put mixture into silicon molds and allow to freeze for 4 hours.

3. Once frozen, put treat into Ziploc bags and store in the freezer.

Pineapple Yoghurt Treat

This contains iron and copper for strong and healthy bones.

Preparation time: 10 minutes

Cooking time: 0 minutes

Servings: 4

Ingredients:

2/3 cup Greek yogurt

1 1/2 cups cubed pineapple

Directions:

1. Blend pineapple until smooth

2. Add yogurt and blend, until thoroughly mixed.

3. Pour mixture into a silicon mold.

4. Put the mold in your freezer for 3 hours, or until they become hard.

GRAIN FREE TREATS

Pumpkin Salmon Treat

This helps to control parasites on your dog.

Preparing time: 2 minutes

Cooking time: 20 minutes

Servings: 4

Ingredients:

1/2 cup pumpkin puree

4 eggs

1/2 cup melted coconut oil

1 1/2 cups coconut flour

1 cup canned salmon, drained

2 tablespoons fresh parsley, roughly chopped (optional)

Directions:

1. Pulse all ingredients in a food processor until thoroughly blended and can be rolled into a ball with your hands. If you think it's too wet, mix in a little more coconut four.

2. Using your hands, carefully flatten the ball into the shape of a disc.

3. Cover with plastic wrap and refrigerate for 1-2 hours.

4. Preheat oven to 350F.

5. Arrange parchment paper on two baking sheets.

6. Place dough between two parchment papers and roll out into 1/8 – 1/4 inch thickness.

7. Use cookie cutter to cut dough into desired shapes. Gather scraps, flatten and cut also.

8. Bake for 18 - 20 minutes or until treat is hard and golden brown.

9. Let cool then transfer to an airtight container. It can be stored for up to three weeks.

Coconut Pumpkin Dog Treat

Helps improve the respiratory health of dogs.

Preparation time: 5 minutes

Cooking time: 45 minutes

Servings: 10

Ingredients:

1 teaspoon cinnamon

1 2/3 cups of coconut flour

1 teaspoon turmeric

1/2 cup melted coconut oil

1 (15 oz.) can pumpkin

1/2 cup creamy peanut butter

4 eggs

Directions:

1. Preheat oven to 350°F.

2. In a large bowl, whisk the peanut butter, coconut oil, pumpkin and eggs properly, set aside.

3. Add the coconut flour, turmeric and cinnamon.

4. Stir until they are properly combined.

5. Allow dough to sit for 10 minutes to allow proper absorption by the coconut flour.

6. Scoop spoonfuls of dough onto a greased baking pan and press down with a fork.

7. Bake for 45 minutes or until the top is browned.

Sweet Potato & Salmon Treat

This helps to prevent urinary inconsistency.

Preparing time: 5 minutes

Cooking time: 30 minutes

Servings: 4

Ingredients:

1/2 teaspoon baking powder

1/4 cup fresh parsley, chopped

2 cups sweet potato (dry mashed with no added milk or water)

2 cups canned salmon, mashed

1 egg

1 1/2 cups garbanzo bean flour

Directions:

1. Preheat oven to 350°F.

2. In a large bowl, mix together sweet potato and salmon.

3. Add the egg, baking powder, parsley and stir thoroughly.

4. Sieve in bean flour a bit at a time, while frequently stirring until dough is firm but not too sticky.

5. With hands, roll the dough into 1/4 – 1/2-inch balls.

6. Place them on a cookie pan and press them down with your thumb.

7. Bake for 25 - 30 minutes until the bottom s start to brown.

Chickpea Pumpkin Treats
Made out of three healthy ingredients

Preparation time: 20 minutes

Cooking time: 30 minutes

Servings: 2

Ingredients:

1/2 cup pumpkin puree

1 1/2 cups chickpea flour

1/2 cup peanut butter

Directions:

1. Preheat oven to 350°F.

2. Mix all ingredients in a larger bowl and mix to form a dough ball. If it is sticky, mix in a few teaspoons of chickpea flour until it is no longer sticky.

3. Wrap up the dough with plastic wrap, place in the fridge and let it sit for an hour.

4. Line a baking pan with a parchment paper.

5. Sprinkle chickpea flour generously on your counter and a rolling pin. Take the dough out and roll it to 1/4 – 1/2- inch thickness.

6. Use a cookie cutter to cut out the shapes you want and place on the lined baking sheet with 1/2 inch between.

7. Bake for 30 minutes. Switch off the oven but leave the cookies there for additional 15 minutes to dry out. Transfer to a rack to cool completely.

8. Store in an airy place for up to 2 months.

Coconut Banana Dog Treat

This provides natural support for dog fur.

Preparation time: 5 minutes

Cooking time: 20 minutes

Servings: 15

Ingredients:

1 tablespoon honey

1 large banana, mashed

1 tablespoon melted coconut oil

1/2 cup almond milk

2 eggs

1 cup coconut flour

1/3 cup peanut butter

Directions:

1. Preheat oven 300°F.

2. Combine the peanut butter, egg, honey, banana, and coconut oil properly in a bowl.

3. Slowly add the coconut flour and almond milk and stir thoroughly until well combined.

4. Scoop the dough with 1 tablespoon at a time and place on the baking tray.

5. Bake for 20-25 minutes. Transfer to wire rack to cool.

Minty Grain Free Treat

This makes your dog's breath fresh.

Preparation time: 5 minutes

Cooking time: 15 minutes

Servings: 12

Ingredients:

1/2 cup coconut flour

1 egg

3 tablespoons melted coconut oil

3 tablespoons dried parsley

2 tablespoons dried mint

Directions:

1. Preheat oven to 350°F. Place parchment paper on a baking sheet.

2. Mix together all the ingredients.

3. Scoop a little of the batter and roll into a 1/2 inch ball. Place the ball on the baking sheet and flatten to about 1/4 inch. Repeat until the batter is used up.

4. Bake for 15 minutes or until hardened.

Spinach Carrot Treat

Helps to maintain your pup's bones.

Preparation time: 10 minutes

Cooking time: 25 minutes

Servings: 3

Ingredients:

1 cup of chopped baby spinach

1 large carrot, peeled, shredded

2 eggs

3 cups almond flour

2/3 cup pumpkin puree

1/4 pure peanut butter

Directions:

1. Preheat oven to 350°F.

2. Stir pumpkin puree, eggs and butter in an electric mixer.

3. Add flour a bit at a time and mix until well combined.

4. Add spinach and carrots; stir properly.

5. Knead the dough into ball then wrap in plastic wrap and place in the fridge for 1 hour.

6. Roll out the dough on a floured surface then use a cookie cutter or knife to cut out preferred shapes.

7. Place treats on a baking span that you have lined with parchment paper.

8. Bake for 25 minutes or until edges are golden brown.

Bacon Treats

This will get their tails wagging non-stop.

Preparation time: 5 minutes

Cooking time: 15 minutes

Servings: 20

Ingredients:

2 - 3 slices of bacon, cooked, diced

1 1/2 cup coconut flour

1/2 cup coconut oil, melted

1/2 cup almond butter

5 eggs

1 cup plus 2 tablespoons unsweetened applesauce

Directions:

1. Preheat oven to 350°F and line baking sheet with parchment paper.

2. In a large bowl, combine all the ingredients until dough is formed.

3. Roll out dough to about 1/4 inch thickness.

4. Use a cookie cutter to cut out dough into preferred shape and place on the lined baking sheet.

5. Bake for 15 – 20 minutes.

6. Allow to cool completely and store in an airtight container in the refrigerator.

MEAT FREE TREATS

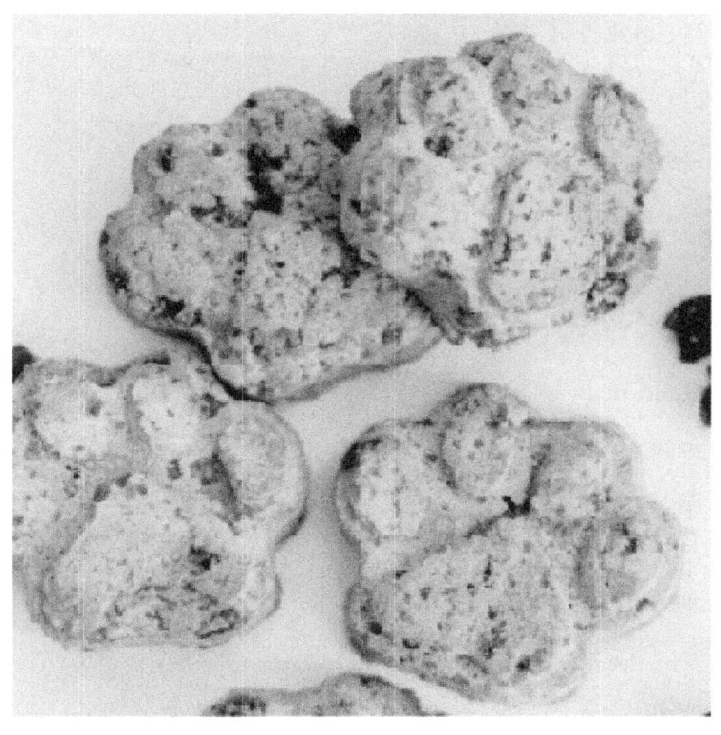

Cranberry Almond Treats

This helps dogs to be more immune to sickness.

Preparation time: 10 minutes

Cooking time: 20 minutes

Servings: 15

Ingredients:

1 cup unblanched almond meal

1/4 cup melted coconut oil

1/4 cup almond milk

1 cup coconut flour

1/3 cup dried cranberries or 1/2 cup of fresh cranberries

1/4 cup almond butter, unsweetened

1 egg

Directions:

1. Preheat oven to 350°F and line a sheet pan with parchment paper.

2. In a large bowl, mix coconut flour and almond meal and set aside.

3. In a small bowl, combine the almond butter, coconut oil, egg and almond milk; stir until well combined.

4. Mix dry ingredients and wet ingredients together.

5. Add cranberries to the mixture and knead until a dough is formed.

6. Place dough on a wax paper and flatten with hands to 1/2-inch thickness.

7. Use a cookie cutter to cut dough into desired shapes.

8. Bake treats for 20 minutes. Take it out of the oven and let cool completely.

Pumpkin Rice Dog Treat

Don't let a day go by without your dog's apple treat.

Preparation time: 10 minutes

Cooking time: 14 minutes

Servings: 25

Ingredients:

1/4 cup powdered coconut milk

1 teaspoon ground turmeric

1/4 cup nutritional yeast

1 tablespoon ground flax seed

1/2 cup pumpkin puree

1 1/4 cups brown rice flour

1 egg

Directions:

1. Preheat oven to 350⁰F.

2. Line a baking sheet with parchment paper.

3. Add the yeast, flax seed, pumpkin puree, egg and milk powder into a large bowl and mix properly with a wooden spoon.

4. Stir in the turmeric.

5. Slowly add flour, a bit at a time, and stir between additions to ensure it is mixed well.

6. Knead properly using your hands to form a dough that is not too sticky.

7. Place dough between two wax papers then roll out dough to 1/4- inch thickness.

8. Use cookie cutter to cut dough to preferred shape.

9. Bake for 14 minutes.

10. Remove from oven and allow to completely cool.

11. Put treats in an airtight jar and store in your refrigerator for up to 10 days.

Turmeric Vegetables Treat

This is great for the cardiovascular system of dogs.

Preparation time: 5 minutes

Cooking time: 35 minutes

Servings: 10

Ingredients:

1 teaspoon baking powder

1/4 cup plain yogurt

1/4 teaspoon turmeric powder

3/4 cup oat flour, sieved

1 cup fresh spinach, chopped finely

1/4 cup fresh parsley, chopped finely

1/2 cup unsweetened applesauce

1 cup carrot, roughly grated

1 1/2 cups brown rice flour, sieved

Directions:

1. Preheat Oven to 325°F.

2. Line a sheet pan with parchment paper and set aside.

3. Add oat flour, baking powder and rice flour into a medium bowl, stir to combine then set aside.

4. Add applesauce, parsley, carrot and spinach into a separate bowl, and stir until well combined.

5. Add yoghurt to vegetable mixture and stir properly. Sprinkle turmeric on top and stir it in.

6. Working one cup at a time, add the mixture of flours into the vegetable mixture. Stirring as you add until all flour is added.

7. Once flour is well mixed, knead with hand to form a dough.

8. If the dough is sticky, sprinkle a little more flour on it and knead it in.

9. Put the dough between 2 wax sheets on a smooth surface and roll to 1/4 thickness.

10. Use a cookie cutter to cut treats into preferred shape.

11. Bake for 35 minutes. Take it out of the oven and let cool completely.

12. It can be stored in the fridge for up to 10 days.

Carrot Oatmeal Treats

Infuses dogs with vitality.

Preparation time: 2 minutes

Cooking time: 14 minutes

Servings: 7

Ingredients:

1/2 cup water

1/2 cup unsalted peanut butter

1 1/2 cups all-purpose flour

2 teaspoons baking powder

1/2 cup unsweetened instant oatmeal

1 cup grated carrot

2 tablespoons dates, pit removed, finely chopped

Directions:

1. Preheat Oven to 325°F.

2. Using a mixing bowl, mix together baking powder, oat meal and flour. Make a well in the middle and keep aside.

3. Add together peanut butter, water, carrot and dates in a separate bowl.

4. Pour the carrot mixture into the flour well then stir until dough is formed.

5. Place the dough on a lightly floured surface and roll to 1/4 inch thickness.

6. Use cookie cutters to cut treats into shapes.

7. Place on cookie sheet lined with parchment paper.

8. Bake for 14 – 16 minutes.

9. Allow the treat to cool, before serving your dog. It can be stored in the fridge for up to 2 weeks.

Simple Grain-Free Treat

So easily made with only 3 easy ingredients!

Preparation time: 5 minutes

Cooking time: 0 minutes

Servings: 10

Ingredients:

3 tablespoons of peanut butter

2 ripe bananas, mashed

3 tablespoons coconut oil, melted

Directions:

1. Place all ingredients in a bowl and mix until almost smooth.

2. Scoop heaped tablespoons of the batter into silicon molds and freeze for about 2 - 3 hours.

Banana Blueberry Treat

Preparation time: 5 minutes

Cooking time: 30 minutes

Servings 4

Ingredients:

1/2 cup unsweetened applesauce

1 medium banana

1/2 cup fresh blueberries, or frozen

1/4 cup ground flaxseed

2 1/2 cups buckwheat flour

2 tablespoons instant goat's milk

Directions:

1. Preheat oven to 350°F.

2. Line sheet pans with parchment paper.

3. Pulse together applesauce, blueberry and banana in a blender until smooth.

4. Pour mixture into a bowl.

5. Add goat's milk, flaxseed and buckwheat flour; stir until thoroughly combined.

6. Knead to form a stiff dough. You may need to add a little water.

7. Roll the dough on a floured surface into 1/4 inch thickness.

8. Cut treats with a cookie cutter and place on prepared sheet pans.

9. Bake for 30 minutes. Transfer to racks to cool.

Peanut Butter Pumpkin Treats

This is absolutely nutritious!

Preparation time:10 minutes

Cooking time: 50 minutes

Servings: 10

Ingredients:

2 cups whole wheat flour

1 egg

4 tablespoons honey

1/3 cup water

1/2 cup peanut butter

1/2 cup canned pumpkin

Directions:

1. Preheat oven to 300°F.

2. In a large bowl, mix together pumpkin, egg, water, peanut butter and honey thoroughly.

3. Slowly add flour to the mixture.

4. Knead with hand or beat with a mixer until you get a firm dough.

5. Place dough on a flat surface, and roll to 1/4-inch thickness.

6. Using a cookie cutters, cut treat to preferred shape.

7. Place the treats on a baking tray and bake for 50 – 60 minutes.

8. Switch off the oven and leave the cookies there for 2-3 hours before removing. This will make them chewier.

LOW FAT TREATS

Veggie Treats

This is good for dogs that are getting too fat.

Preparing time: 5 minutes

Cooking time: 25 minutes

Servings: 5

Ingredients:

1 cup cooked vegetables (zucchini, sweet potatoes or squash)

1 teaspoon dried parsley

7 tablespoons low-fat vegetable broth

2 1/2 cups of rice flour

1/2 cup cold water

Directions:

1. Preheat oven to 350ºF.

2. In a large bowl, mix together the rice flour and dried parsley. Set aside.

3. Add the cooked vegetables, water and vegetable broth to a separate bowl. Stir with a wooden spoon to combine.

4. Gently pour the wet ingredients into the dry ingredients.

5. Mix and knead the batter with your hands until the dough is smooth.

6. Use a rolling pin to roll out the dough until it is flattened.

7. Use a cookie cutter to cut out the treats.

8. Place the treats on a baking sheet you have sprayed with cooking spray.

9. Bake for 25 minutes or until it turns golden.

Low Fat Carrot Treats

Keeps dogs fit and in shape.

Preparation time: 10 minutes

Cooking time: 25 minutes

Servings: 8

Ingredients:

1 medium ripe banana

1/8 cup water

1 cup shredded carrot

1 1/2 cups whole wheat flour

1 cup rolled oats

1/4 cup unsweetened apple juiced

Directions:

1. Preheat oven to 350°F.

2. Lightly spray cooking spray on a baking sheet.

3. Mash the banana in a medium bowl and mix with the shredded carrot.

4. Add water and apple juice to the mixture in the bowl and mix properly.

5. Add flour and rolled oats into the bowl. Stir everything together until they are well combined.

6. Using your hands, knead the mixture to form a dough.

7. Turn the dough onto a lightly floured surface and roll to 1/4-inch thickness.

8. Using a cookie cutter, cut the treat to your preferred shape.

9. Place the cut pieces onto the sprayed baking sheet and bake for 25minutes.

Pumpkin Spinach Biscuit

Your furry friend will thank you endlessly for this.

Preparation time: 5 minutes

Cooking time: 40 minutes

Servings: 4

Ingredients:

1/4 teaspoon salt

1/2 cup pumpkin puree

1 tablespoon water

2 3/4 cups whole wheat flour

1/2 cup fresh spinach leaves, sliced

1/4 cup shredded carrot

2 eggs

1/4 teaspoon cinnamon

Directions:

1. Preheat oven to 350°F.

2. In a blender, blend the pumpkin puree, eggs, spinach, salt and water until smooth.

3. Transfer the mixture to a mixing bowl.

4. Add flour, shredded carrot and cinnamon to the mixture.

5. Knead until a dough is formed.

6. Roll the dough on a floured surface to 1/2-inch thickness.

7. Use a dog bone cookie cutters or a pizza cutter to cut out pieces.

8. Place the pieces on a baking sheet lined with parchment paper.

9. Bake for 20 minutes then flip and bake for another 20 minutes.

10. Take the treats out of the oven and let cool completely before serving.

Low Fat Dog Treat
Good for the gum, bones, teeth of your pup.

Preparation time: 10 minutes

Cooking time: 30 minutes

Servings: 7

Ingredients:

1 teaspoon dried parsley

1 tablespoon coconut oil, melted

1 teaspoon dried drill

1 (15oz) can of chickpeas, drained, rinsed

Directions:

1. Preheat oven to 350°F.

2. Put all ingredients into a large bowl.

3. Stir until they are well combined and chickpea is coated evenly.

4. Spread the mixture on a large baking tray.

5. Bake for 30 – 40 minutes or until crunchy.

Spinach Pumpkin Treats

This is great for keeping your dog's weight in check.

Preparation time: 5 minutes

Cooking time: 35 minutes

Servings: 10

Ingredients:

1 cup whole wheat flour

1 tablespoon fresh parsley, chopped finely

1/2 cup fresh spinach, chopped finely

1 teaspoon wheat germ

2 eggs

1/4 teaspoon sea salt

1/2 cup pumpkin puree

Directions:

1. Preheat oven to350°F and line a baking pan with parchment paper.

2. In a small bowl, mix flour and salt then set aside.

3. Put pumpkin puree, spinach, parsley and eggs into a different bowl, and mix properly using a wooden spoon.

4. Add wheat germ into mixture and stir it in.

5. Add the prepared flour from the small bowl into the pumpkin mixture, a little bit at a time, stirring properly to combine between additions.

6. Use hand to knead to form a dough.

7. Put dough on a floured surface or wax paper and roll out to 1/4-inch thickness.

8. Using a cookie cutter, cut out treats.

9. Bake for 30 - 35 minutes.

10. Transfer treats to an airtight container and store for up to 1 week in the pantry or 2 weeks in the fridge.

Pumpkin Dog Treats

This comes with less fat to prevent weight gain which is ideal for older dogs.

Preparation time: 5 minutes

Cooking time 18 minutes

Servings: 4

Ingredients:

1 cup pumpkin puree

1/2 cup applesauce

3 1/2 cups flour

1 egg

Directions:

1. Set oven to 350°F.

2. In a medium bowl, thoroughly combine all the ingredients except the flour.

3. Add the flour and mix until dough is formed.

4. Sprinkle a little flour on a pastry board or flat surface.

5. Place dough on the board and roll dough to 1/8 thickness.

6. Use any size of cookie cutter to cut out preferred shapes.

7. Place the treats on a baking sheet and bake for 18 minutes.

8. Let the treats cool before serving.

Zucchini Crisps

This has high antioxidants that are healthy for your dog's skin.

Preparation time: 10 minutes

Cooking time: 8 hours

Servings: 4

Ingredients:

2 or 3 zucchini, washed, sliced thinly

2 heaped tablespoons of freeze dried meat treats

Directions:

1. Use a dehydrator or preheat oven to 150°F.

2. Add freeze dried meat to a plastic bag and pound with a mallet to crush as much as possible.

3. Add the sliced zucchini to the bag then shake to coat the slices with the crushed dried meat.

4. Arrange the zucchini on a baking sheet or on the trays of your dehydrator.

5. Bake for 8 to 12 hours or until crispy and fully dried.

6. Keep in an airtight container.

CAKES

Banana Cake

Easy and no stress!

Preparation time: 10minutes

Cooking time: 45

Servings: 4

Ingredients:

2 ripe bananas

1/2 cup creamy peanut butter

4 tablespoons of coconut oil, melted

1 teaspoon baking powder

1 teaspoon baking soda

1 cup unsweetened oat milk

1 large carrot, grated

2 cups of oat flour

2 eggs

Directions:

1. Preheat the oven to 350°F. Grease a 7x10-inch cake pan with coconut oil.

2. Combine your peanut butter, bananas, and coconut oil in a large bowl, and mix properly.

3. Add in the eggs and stir to combine.

4. Sieve in the baking powder, the oat flour, baking soda, and properly stir until well combined.

5. Carefully pour in the oat milk and mix it in.

6. Stir in the grated carrot.

7. Scoop batter into the greased cake pan.

8. Bake for 40 – 45 minutes. Test doneness with a toothpick.

Coconut Berry Dog cake
This treat is rich in Vitamin C and good for dog bones.

Preparation: 5 minutes

Cooking time: 25 minutes

Servings: 2

Ingredients:

3 tablespoon of melted coconut oil

2 tablespoon of honey

1/4 cup of blueberries

1 1/2 cups of coconut floor

2 eggs

For frosting:

3/4 cup plain yoghurt

2 tablespoon of honey, optional

Natural food coloring, optional

Blueberries and strawberries, for toping

Directions

1. Preheat oven to 350°F.

2. Grease a 4-inch springform cake pan with oil and set aside.

3. In a large bowl, thoroughly mix eggs, honey and coconut oil.

4. Add the blueberries and coconut flour, then stir until they are well combined and smooth.

5. Scoop the mixture into your cake pan, and bake for about 25 minutes.

6. For frosting, mix together the coloring, yogurt and honey until they well combined.

7. Once cake is done and has cooled to room temperature, cover with the frosting and top with berries.

Birthday Cake
This is quite easy to make.

Preparation time: 10 minutes

Cooking time: 20 minutes

Servings: 1

Ingredients:

1/2 apple, chopped finely

1/2 teaspoon baking powder

1 large egg, beaten lightly

3 tablespoons of peanut butter

Directions:

1. Preheat oven to350°F. Spray cooking spray on a ramekin or cake pan.

2. In a medium bowl, add together sieved baking powder and peanut butter, mix thoroughly until well combined.

3. Mix in the egg and sliced apple.

4. Pour the batter into the greased cake pan or ramekin, and bake for about 20 minutes. Test doneness with a toothpick.

5. Allow the cake to cool then serve your dog!

Carrot Peanut Butter Cake

It is packed with healthy nutrients for your beloved dog.

Preparation time: 15 minutes

Cooking time: 20 minutes

Servings: 5

Ingredients:

1 cup grated carrots

1/3 cup of honey

1 egg

1/4 cup peanut butter

1 teaspoon of baking soda

1 cup whole wheat flour

1/4 cup coconut oil

Frosting:

1/2 cup of Greek yogurt

1/2 cup peanut butter

1banana, for topping

Directions:

1. Preheat oven to 350°F. Grease a round 9-inch cake pan.

2. In a bowl, mix the peanut butter, egg, coconut oil, and honey thoroughly until smooth.

3. Gradually sieve in flour and baking soda into the bowl, and mix until they are well combined.

4. Add the grated carrot and stir.

5. Put the mixture into the greased cake pan, and let it bake for 20 minutes. Test doneness with a toothpick.

6. When done, transfer to a rack to cool completely.

7. Prepare the frosting by mixing the yoghurt and peanut butter in a bowl. Spread this mixture on cake and top with chopped banana.

Bacon Fat Dog Cake

This treat is for bone strengthening!

Preparation time: 10 minutes

Cooking time: 25 minutes

Servings: 4

Ingredients:

2 tablespoons of honey

1/4 cup peanut butter

2 eggs

1 cup unbleached flour

1/2 cup unsweetened applesauce

1/2 cup unsweetened pumpkin puree

3 tablespoons of bacon fat

1 teaspoon of baking soda

Directions:

1. Preheat oven to 350°F. Grease a round 8-inch cake pan and place parchment paper in it.

2. Cook the bacon slices in a pan until it is crisp. Reserve the bacon fat.

3. In a large bowl, put in 3 tablespoon of the bacon fat, together with the peanut butter, pumpkin puree, honey and apple sauce then mix thoroughly.

4. Add eggs, sieved flour and baking soda into the batter bowl and mix properly until well-combined. Don't mix too much.

5. Transfer the batter into the greased pan and bake for 25 - 30 minutes or until a tooth pick inserted comes out clean.

Carrot Sweet Potato Cake

This cake gives dogs a lot of happy energy.

Preparation time: 5 minutes

Cooking time: 30 minutes

Servings: 3

Ingredients:

1/4 cup of water

1 cup flour

1/2 cup pureed sweet potato

3 tablespoons of vegetable oil

1 teaspoon of baking powder

2 tablespoons honey

1 teaspoon baking powder

1/2 cup grated carrot

For frosting:

1/4 cup sweet potato puree

1/4 cup plain yogurt

A sprinkling of grated carrot

Directions:

1. Preheat oven to 350°F.

2. Combine the oil, sweet potatoes and honey in a large bowl and mix thoroughly.

3. Add in the remaining ingredients and stir until the consistency is uniform.

4. Pour the mixture into a round or square cake pan and bake for 30 minutes.

5. For frosting, mix the Greek yoghurt and sweet potato puree nicely.

6. When the cake is completely cooled, spread the frosting on it and top with grated carrots.

Pumpkin Cake

Show your dog you adore them with this yummy cake.

Preparation time: 5 minutes

Cooking time: 25 minutes

Servings: 3

Ingredients:

1 cup of flour

1/2 cup pure pumpkin puree

1/2 cup plain unsweetened applesauce

1/8 cup vegetable oil

1/2 teaspoon baking soda

1 egg

1/4 cup natural peanut butter

Frosting:

1/4 cup peanut butter

1/2 cup plain Greek yogurt

Directions:

1. Preheat oven on 350°F degrees. Coat a round 8-inch pan with oil.

2. In a large bowl, combine the baking soda and flour.

3. In another bowl, thoroughly mix the vegetable oil, peanut butter, pumpkin puree and applesauce.

4. Add the egg to the applesauce mixture and mix it in.

5. Add the wet ingredients to the dry ingredients; stir until well-combined.

6. Put the batter into the prepared pan.

7. Bake for 25 to 30 minutes or until the cake springs back when pressed gently. Test doneness with a toothpick.

8. For the frosting, mix together the Greek yogurt and peanut butter until smooth.

9. When the cake is completely cooled, spread the frosting on it.

ICING AND DIPS

Easy Icing

Decorate your dog's treats with this simple icing recipe.

Preparation time: 5 minutes

Cooking time: 0 minutes

Servings: 4

Ingredients:

1/2 cup plain Greek yogurt

1/2 cup tapioca starch

1 tablespoon milk

Food coloring, optional

Direction:

1. Combine tapioca starch and yogurt in a mixing bowl then stir thoroughly to get a creamy mixture.

2. Slowly pour the milk into mixture, mixing as you pour.

3. Mix until it has the consistency of icing. If it is too soft, add more tapioca flour.

4. Add in food coloring if you like.

5. Use this icing to decorate treats ad then place in the refrigerator to harden.

Banana Yogurt Dip

Preparation time: 3 minutes

Cooking time: 0 minutes

Servings: 10

Ingredients:

1/4 cup plain Greek yogurt

1/2 banana, mashed

2 tablespoons peanut butter, optional

Directions:

1. Mix all the ingredients until smooth and creamy.

2. Serve with any treat or cookies.

3. Cover and store in the refrigerator.

Rice Flour Icing

Preparation time: 5 minutes

Cooking time: 0 minutes

Servings: 4

Ingredients:

1 teaspoon honey

2 teaspoons water

2 tablespoons rice flour or cornstarch

Food coloring, optional

Directions:

1. Add rice flour to medium bowl.

2. Add water to the flour and mix it in. Add honey and whisk until thoroughly combined. Add more water if necessary.

3. Stir in food coloring.

4. Use to decorate dog treats.

Peanut Butter Carob Dip

Preparation time: 3 minutes

Cooking time: 0 minutes

Servings: 5

Ingredients:

1/4 cup natural peanut butter

1/4 cup Carob drops

Directions:

1. Mix both ingredients together in a microwaveable bowl.

2. Microwave on medium heat while stirring to combine.

3. Allow to cool, and serve with any cookie or treat.

Cream Cheese Frosting

Preparation time: 3 minutes

Cooking time: 0 minutes

Servings: 10

Ingredients:

1 tablespoon pure pumpkin

1 (4.oz) package of low fat cream cheese, room temperature

Directions:

1. Combine the ingredients until thoroughly smooth and creamy.

2. Once icing is made, cover and store in the refrigerator.

Cheese Yogurt Icing

Preparation time: 5 minutes

Cooking time: 0 minutes

Servings: 8

Ingredients:

10 tablespoons plain Greek Yogurt, room temperature

1 cup cream cheese, room temperature

Directions:

1. Combine the ingredients in a mixing bowl and use a hand or stand mixer to mix thoroughly.

2. Spread on cooled cookies or cake.

Peanut Butter Frosting

Preparation time: 5 minutes

Cooking time: 0 minutes

Servings: 12

Ingredients:

8 ounces cream cheese, room temperature

1 cup smooth peanut butter

Directions:

1. In a bowl, whisk together the cream cheese and peanut butter until creamy and smooth.

2. Spread on dog cakes or dog cupcakes.

CHEWY TREATS

Soft Chew
Dogs love to chew on this treat all day.

Preparation time: 10 minutes

Cooking time: 25 minutes

Servings: 20

Ingredients:

2 cups whole wheat flour

1/4 cup water

1 teaspoon baking powder

1 cup natural peanut butter

2 bananas, mashed

Directions:

1. Preheat oven to 350°F.

2. Combine peanut butter and banana in a medium bowl and mix until combined.

3. Add water, baking powder and flour to the mixture; knead until a dough is formed.

4. Roll dough out to 1/4 inch thickness.

5. Using a cookie cutter, cut batter to desired shape.

6. Place treat on a baking sheet lined with parchment paper.

7. Bake for 10 minutes, flip and bake for an extra 10 – 15 minutes.

8. Serve when completely cool.

Milky Dog Chew

This will keep your dog busy for some time.

Preparation time: 5 minutes

Cooking time: 40 minutes

Servings: 40

Ingredients:

1 teaspoon sea salt

1 gallon skim milk

1/2 cup lime juice

Directions:

1. Place a pot on medium heat and pour in the skim milk, stirring until it boils. Turn off the heat.

2. Add the remaining ingredients to the milk.

3. Gently stir for about 1 – 2 minutes or until the whey starts separating from the curd. Set aside without stirring for 10 – 15 minutes.

4. Drape a large bowl with cheese cloth and drain out the liquid leaving the curds.

5. Twist the cloth and squeeze to drain out more liquid. Squeeze as hard as you can.

6. Apply pressure, by placing any heavy object on the dish cloth to completely drain out liquid for up to 6 hours.

7. Discard the dish cloth and cut the solid mixture into desired shapes. Place on baking pan.

8. Preheat oven to 150°F, bake for 40 minutes.

9. Allow to cool on a rack and dry completely for about 24 hours before you serve.

Sweet Chew

Preparation time: 10 minutes

Cooking time: 2 ½ hours

Servings: 5

Ingredients:

Cinnamon

1 large sweet potato

1 1/2 tablespoons olive oil

Instructions:

1. Preheat oven to 250°F.

2. Cut potato into long strips of about 1/4 inch thickness.

3. Sprinkle olive oil on the potato strips and toss.

4. Spread out potato strips on a lined baking sheet.

5. Add a sprinkling of cinnamon.

6. Bake for 2 1/2 - 3 hours.

7. Allow to cool and store in an airtight container in your fridge for up to 3 weeks. It can stay in the freezer for up to 4 months.

Banana Chew

Preparation time: 10 minutes

Cooking time: 1 1/2 hour

Servings: 1 - 2

Ingredients:

5 -10 bananas, peeled, halved lengthwise

Lemon juice, optional

Honey, optional

Directions:

1. Preheat oven to 210°F.

2. Line baking sheet with parchment paper. Spread out the banana slices on the baking sheet.

3. Brush lemon juice on the banana slices to keep from browning.

4. Bake for 1 1/2 hours.

5. Bring the treats out of the oven and drizzle with honey.

Cheddar Carrot Chew

This enjoyably chewy treat also aids digestion.

Preparation time: 5 minutes

Cooking time: 12 minutes

Servings: 4

Ingredients:

1/2 cup shredded cheddar cheese

1/2 cup unsweetened Greek yogurt

1/3 cup water

2 cups whole wheat flour

1 egg, lightly whisked

1 cup old-fashioned oatmeal

2 teaspoons baking powder

1/2 cup grated carrot

Directions:

1. Preheat oven to 325°F. Place parchment paper on 2 baking sheets.

2. In a bowl, mix baking powder and flour thoroughly.

3. Add yoghurt, cheddar, oatmeal, carrot, and 1/2 of the flour mixture to a mixer bowl. Mix together on low speed, gradually mixing in the rest of the flour mixture.

5. Drizzle in the water and egg then mix until batter is well combined.

6. Scoop 1 teaspoon of the mixture at a time, roll with hands to form a ball then place on the parchment paper-lined baking sheet. Slightly flatten the balls with a fork.

7. Bake for 12 minutes or until browned lightly on the outside and soft on the inside.

8. Remove from the oven and allow treats to cool on racks. Store in the fridge for a few days or for longer in the freezer.

Pumpkin Apple Chew

Preparation time: 10 minutes

Cooking time: 6 hours

Servings: 20

Ingredients:

1 cup applesauce

1/2 tablespoon cinnamon

1 cup pure pumpkin puree

Directions:

1. Preheat oven to 175°F.

2. Mix all ingredients in a large bowl, until properly combined.

3. Line a baking pan with parchment paper.

4. Using a spoon, form long thick lines of batter on the pan. Don't make the lines too thick for faster drying.

5. Bake for 6 – 7 hours until firm. Make sure to check every hour.

6. Take them out of the oven and let cool for a little when then use scissors to cut the strips to desired length. You can also twist them to make spirals.

7. Serve!

Apple Chew

This requires just one ingredient!

Preparation time: 5 minutes

Cooking time: 1 hour

Servings: 4

Ingredients:

4 apples, cored and thinly sliced

Directions:

1. Preheat oven to 210°F.

2. Pat dry the apple slices with a kitchen towel.

3. Place the slices on baking sheet, lined with parchment paper.

4. Bake for an hour, flip sides then bake for an additional hour.

5. Switch off the oven and let the apple treat stay in the oven until completely cooled.

6. Store in an airtight container.

Banana Bread Chew

Let your pup have this when it has been good.

Preparation time: 5 minutes

Cooking time: 35 minutes

Servings: 8

Ingredients:

1 banana, mashed

1/2 cup pumpkin puree

1 tablespoon coconut oil

1 tablespoon ground flaxseed

2 large eggs

1/2 cup coconut flour

Directions:

1. Preheat oven to 350°F.

2. Place parchment paper on a baking sheet.

3. Whisk together flaxseed and coconut flour in a medium bowl

4. In another bowl, mix together the pumpkin puree, banana, egg and coconut oil.

5. Use a spoon to combine the dry ingredients and wet ingredients thoroughly until you have a thick batter.

6. Scoop the batter onto the prepared baking sheet and spread it out to form a layer of about 1/4 inch thickness. Leave it to set for about 5 minutes.

7. Using a knife, create little squares on the batter.

8. Bake for 35 minutes and allow to cool on wire rack.

9. Once cooled, break the treats into squares.

END

Thank you for reading my book. If you enjoyed it, won't you please take a moment to leave me a good review at your retailer?

Thanks!

Heidi Green

Made in the USA
Las Vegas, NV
22 November 2022